CELLS
& LIFE

The World of the Cell

Life on a small scale

Robert Snedden

Heinemann
LIBRARY

www.heinemann.co.uk
Visit our website to find out more information about Heinemann Library books.

TO ORDER:
 Phone 44 (0) 1865 888066
 Send a fax to 44 (0) 1865 314091
Visit the Heinemann Bookshop at **www.heinemann.co.uk** to browse our catalogue and order online.

First published in Great Britain by Heinemann Library, Halley Court, Jordan Hill, Oxford OX2 8EJ, part of Harcourt Education. Heinemann is a registered trademark of Harcourt Education Ltd.

Editorial: Andrew Farrow and Claire Throp
Design: Kimberly R. Miracle and Betsy Wernert
Picture research: Tracy Cummins
Illustrations: Wooden Ark
Production: Alison Parsons
Originated by Chroma Graphics Pte. Ltd
Printed and bound in China by Leo Paper Group

ISBN 978 0 4311 7462 4
12 11 10 09 08
10 9 8 7 6 5 4 3 2 1

British Library Cataloguing in Publication Data
Snedden, Robert
The world of the cell: life on a small scale. –
   2nd ed – (Cells and life)
571.6
A full catalogue record for this book is available from the British Library.

Acknowledgements
The publishers would like to thank the following for permission to reproduce photographs: Corbis p. **41** (R White); Corbis/Royalty-Free p. **30**; Photodisc p. **31**; Science Photo Library pp. **19**, **32** (M. Abbey), **7**, **16**, **35** (J. Burgess), **14** (M. F. Chillmaid), **24** (E. Grave), **25** (M. Kage), **27** (K. H. Kjeldsen), **20** (B. Longcore), **33** (K. Lounatmaa), **12** (G. Murti), **5**, **42** (A. Pasieka), **37** (D. Patterson), **43** (M. Rohde, gbf), **26**, **39** top, **39** bottom (A. Syred); Science Photo Library/Biozentrum, University of Basel p. **37**; Science Photo Library/Eye of Science pp. **15**, **28**; Science Photo Library/Universite D'ancon, CNRI p. **9** (S. Cinti); Science Photo Library/UCT p. **34** (I. Itannard).

Cover photograph of a scanning electron micrograph of *Acinetobacter* sp., a gram-negative rod, and coccobacillus prokaryote, reproduced with permission of Phototake/Dennis Kunkel.

Our thanks to Richard Fosbery for his comments in the preparation of this book, and also to Alexandra Clayton.

Every effort has been made to contact copyright holders of any material reproduced in this book. Any omissions will be rectified in subsequent printings if notice is given to the Publisher.

Disclaimer
All the Internet addresses (URLs) given in this book were valid at the time of going to press. However, due to the dynamic nature of the Internet, some addresses may have changed, or sites may have ceased to exist since publication. While the author and publishers regret any inconvenience this may cause readers, no responsibility for any such changes can be excepted by either the author or the publishers.

Contents

Some words are shown in bold, **like this**. You can find the definitions for these words in the glossary.

All life is cells

Living cells are amazing things. A single cell is too small for us to see without the help of a **microscope**, and yet this tiny package of chemicals has all the properties of life. Cells are the units of life. They are life's building blocks. The simplest forms of life, such as bacteria, are single cells. The more complex plants and animals we see around us – including humans – are built from great assemblies of cells, millions upon millions of them all working together. In fact, there are around 65 million million cells in the human body.

A cell is not a simple unchanging structure. It is a living, dynamic thing that carries out many different jobs. Cells can grow and reproduce, they respond to changes in their environment, and they adapt to changing conditions.

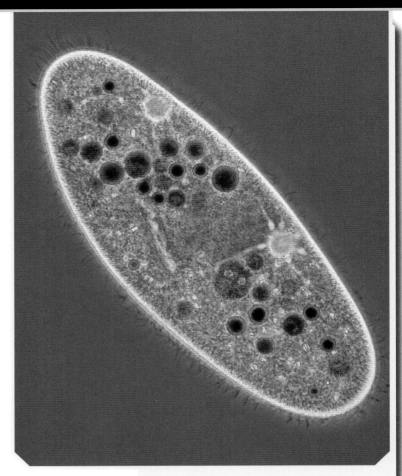

The simplest forms of life are single cells. *Paramecium* is a single-celled creature that is part of a group called **protistans**. It feeds on other protistans. Magnification approx. x 1,000.

Cell theory

Cell theory grew from studies of the cell carried out by scientists in the 19th century. Its three points still hold true today.

1   Every **organism** is composed of one or more cells.
2   The cell is the smallest unit that has the properties of life.
3   All life arises from the growth and division of single cells.

"Little rooms"

In 1665 Robert Hooke, a scientist working in London, used a microscope that he had built himself to examine thin slices of cork (cork is made from the bark of trees). Hooke's microscope could only magnify objects about 30 times, but this was enough to show a honeycomb-like network of tiny, box-like compartments in the cork. Hooke called these little compartments *cellulae*, from a Latin word meaning "little rooms". From this we get our word cells.

What Hooke saw in the cork were the empty cell walls of dead plant tissue. He had noticed that cells in living plants were filled with what he called "juices", but his microscope was not powerful enough to show any detail of the inside of the cell.

Recipe for a cell

At one time cells were thought to be little more than tiny droplets of living material, called protoplasm. We now know that they are a little more complex than that! All cells have a thin outer **membrane**. Plant cells have a tough cell wall as well as a membrane. Between 70 and 80 per cent of a cell's weight is water, but along with this there is also a mind-bogglingly complex "soup" made up of many different substances. Vast numbers of chemical reactions are going on in this soup all the time, as substances are arranged and rearranged, broken apart and joined together again in different ways.

Cells are made from several basic ingredients that are essential to all life. All of them are large **molecules** made from chains of smaller repeating units.

Proteins are part of many cell structures (for instance, membranes), and proteins called **enzymes** control the many chemical reactions in the cell. **Lipids** (fats) are the other main substance in membranes, and they are also used as energy stores. **Carbohydrates** are made from long chains of sugars; they are the cell's main source of energy. **Nucleic acids** such as **DNA** are the cell's genetic material. DNA contains information the cell needs to grow and reproduce.

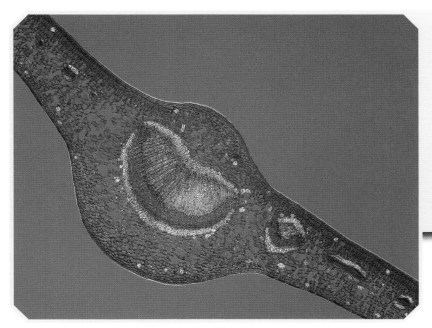

A cross-section of a leaf from an evergreen shrub, seen through a light microscope. The image shows that the leaf is made up of thousands of cells. The pinkish areas are the leaf veins. The cells here are specialized to carry water and nutrients around the plant. Magnification approx. x 40.

Cell shapes and sizes

How small is a cell? Many are very small indeed. Measuring cells using everyday units such as metres would be hopeless. A red blood cell, for example, is about 8 millionths of a metre across. One millionth of a metre is a micrometre. A typical plant or animal cell is between 5 and 20 micrometres across. An average bacterium is even smaller, just 1 or 2 micrometres across.

However, a few types of cell are big enough to be seen with the naked eye. The inside of a bird's egg, for example, is really a single cell; and some nerve cells, such as those in the neck of a giraffe, can be over a metre in length.

But why are most cells so small? Why don't living things have a few big cells, instead of millions of small ones?

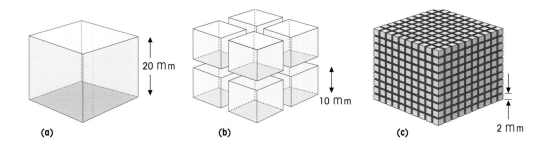

	Length of one side (Mm = micrometres)	Volume (length x height x width x no. of cubes)	Surface area (length x width x no. of sides x no. of cubes)
(a)	20 Mm	8,000 Mm³	2,400 Mm²
(b)	10 Mm	8,000 Mm³	4,800 Mm²
(c)	2 Mm	8,000 Mm³	24,000 Mm²

In this diagram, the single cube, the eight smaller cubes, and the 1,000 very small cubes all have the same total volume: 8,000 cubic micrometres. However, the surface area of the 1,000 small cubes is 10 times greater than that of the single cube.

Surface and volume

The main thing that keeps cells so small is surface area to volume ratio. Think of a simple cell as being a tiny cube measuring 10 micrometres on each side. The volume of the cell is 10 x 10 x 10 = 1,000 cubic micrometres, and its surface area is 10 x 10 x 6 = 600 square micrometres. If you double the length of each side to 20 micrometres, then its volume becomes 20 x 20 x 20 = 8,000: not twice, but eight times greater. However, the surface area is 20 x 20 x 6 = 2,400, which is only four times greater. This means that each part of the cell's surface has to transport nutrients and waste in and out of the cell for twice as much of the inside as it did before. The bigger the cell becomes, the more its surface area lags behind its volume. If the cell becomes too big, it becomes impossible for it to get nutrients in and waste out fast enough.

Once inside the cell, nutrients have to be moved to the places where they are needed. In the small-scale world of the cell, there are no veins and arteries to transport materials. Instead, the cell relies on the **diffusion** of **molecules** through its interior. Such a transport system simply does not work once the cell gets beyond a certain size.

For a chemical reaction to take place in a cell (or anywhere else), the chemicals reacting together must come into contact with each other! If a cell doubled in size, it would have to manufacture eight times more chemicals to ensure that reactions took place.

So how is it possible for cells to grow to a metre in length? Well, egg cells can be large because most of the cell is yolk. The yolk is a stored food supply for the growing embryo, which does not need food from any other source. Other big cells are either long and thin, or have many folds and indentations. These shapes act to increase the cell's surface area.

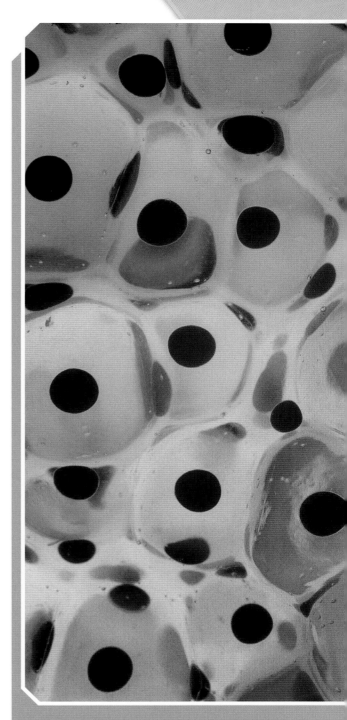

Each egg in this frog spawn is initially a single cell. The cell divides many times as it grows. Magnification approx. x 8.

Cell structure

Cells come in a huge variety of sizes and shapes and carry out a wide range of activities. Yet they all share features in common. All cells have an outer "skin" or **membrane**. Within this membrane, the cell can be divided into two main areas: an area containing the cell's genetic material (**DNA**); and the **cytoplasm**, which contains everything else the cell needs to carry out its normal functions.

Prokaryotes and eukaryotes

At the most basic level, cells can be divided into two types. In one type, the cell's genetic material is surrounded by a membrane, forming a structure called the **nucleus**. Such cells are known as **eukaryotes** (this means "true nucleus"). In the other, simpler cell type, the genetic material is not enclosed by a membrane. Such cells are called **prokaryotes** ("before nucleus"). Bacteria and **archaea** are prokaryotes, while all other cells, including the cells that make up all plants and animals, are eukaryotes. Eukaryote cells are generally bigger than prokaryotes.

Cell walls and membranes

The cell membrane, or **plasma membrane**, is the boundary between the cell and the rest of the world. A cell cannot be completely isolated from its environment, as it needs to take in raw materials from outside the cell and to get rid of the waste products it produces. The cell membrane controls what can come into the cell from outside and what leaves it.

A cell membrane is a double layer of phospholipid **molecules** (fats with a phosphate group on one end). The "tails" of the lipid molecules repel water, and face into the middle of the membrane. Proteins embedded in the membrane act as pathways that allow certain molecules to pass through.

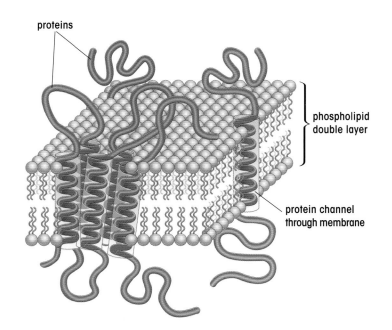

proteins

phospholipid double layer

protein channel through membrane

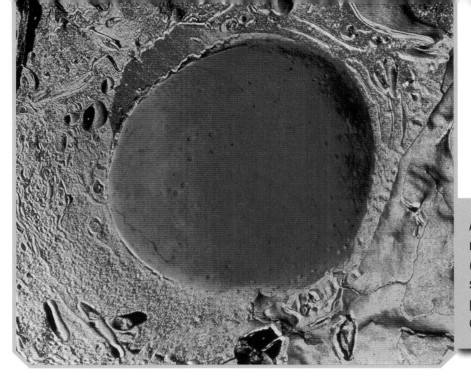

A close-up of a cell's nuclear membrane (or envelope), showing the nuclear pores. Magnification approx. x 15,000.

Some cells, notably those of plants and bacteria, also have a tough external cell wall outside the cell membrane. In plants, this wall is made of **cellulose**. It surrounds the cell and provides protection and strength. Bacteria may have a third layer of protection, a slimy material called the slime capsule.

A cell membrane is selectively, or partially, permeable, meaning that some substances can get in and out, but others cannot. The membrane is made up of a double sheet of **lipid** (fat), with **proteins** embedded in the surface. Some of these proteins provide channels through which some substances can pass in and out of the cell. Other proteins act like pumps, actively moving substances in and out of the cell.

In animals, objects that are too large to pass through the cell membrane can get into the cell by a process called **endocytosis**. The membrane folds around the object to form a small bubble, called a **vesicle**, which passes into the cell.

The nucleus

The nucleus is the central, roughly spherical area in eukaryotes where a cell's genetic material is found. It is surrounded by a double membrane, called the nuclear envelope. Pores (small holes) in the envelope control the passage of molecules in and out of the nucleus. The nucleus contains a complete set of the **organism's** genes. The genes contain instructions for making proteins, which control the way the cell develops and functions.

Cytoplasm

The cytoplasm is everything found between the cell membrane and the nuclear membrane (or envelope). In eukaryotes, the cytoplasm contains a number of different structures, called **organelles**, which do specific jobs within the cell.

2

Inside a eukaryote cell

Eukaryote cells have a more complicated structure than the simple **prokaryotes**. The inside of a eukaryote contains many different structures called **organelles**. Each organelle has a specialized function. Organelles called **mitochondria**, for example, store most of the **enzymes** and other chemicals that the cell needs to get energy from food.

Cutaway views of a typical plant cell and a typical animal cell. Both plant and animal cells are eukaryotes. Unlike animal cells, plant cells have a rigid cell wall and a large sap-filled cavity (the **vacuole**) that fills most of the cell.

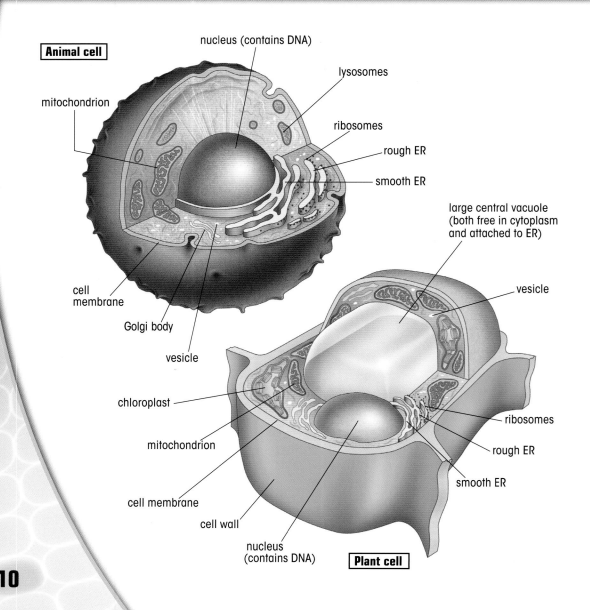

Animal cell

nucleus (contains DNA)

lysosomes

mitochondrion

ribosomes

rough ER

smooth ER

large central vacuole (both free in cytoplasm and attached to ER)

vesicle

cell membrane

Golgi body

vesicle

chloroplast

ribosomes

mitochondrion

rough ER

smooth ER

cell membrane

cell wall

nucleus (contains DNA)

Plant cell

Organelles keep different chemical reactions within the cell separate. Each organelle can bring together and store the various materials it needs to carry out the reactions that take place there. Packaging the chemicals for particular processes in this way allows the cell to operate much more efficiently.

A typical cell

Although a typical animal cell and a typical plant cell are shown in the illustration opposite, in reality there is no such thing as a "typical" cell, any more than there is a typical plant or a typical animal. All cells have the same basic plan, but there are hundreds of variations on the theme. The main features of eukaryote cells are listed in the table below.

Common features of the eukaryote cell

Nucleus	Contains the cell's genetic material, or **DNA**.
Mitochondria	The cell's powerhouses, where energy from food is made available.
Chloroplasts	Organelles found only in plant cells. **Chloroplasts** are where **photosynthesis** takes place. This is the process by which plants make food from sunlight, water, and carbon dioxide from the air.
Ribosome	Tiny, roundish structures where small **molecules** called **amino acids** are joined together to make **proteins**.
Endoplasmic reticulum	A network of **membranes** within the cell. Most of the cell's **ribosomes** are found on the **endoplasmic reticulum (ER)**.
Golgi body	Organelles where the final stages of protein assembly are carried out. Proteins for use outside the cell are completed in the **Golgi body**.
Vesicles	Small membrane sacs that perform a variety of functions, including breaking down (digesting) substances absorbed by the cell.
Tubules and filaments	Tiny tubes and fibres that form a "cell skeleton". The tubules and fibres can contract (shorten). They are important for movement of the whole cell and for cell division.

Within the cytoplasm

As mentioned earlier, the **cytoplasm** is all the parts of a cell between the cell **membrane** and the **nucleus**. All the cell's internal membranes and **organelles**, such as the **mitochondria** and **chloroplasts**, are suspended in a jelly-like material called **cytosol**. In many cells the cytosol and organelles are organized by a microscopic network of **protein** filaments called the **cytoskeleton**.

The cell skeleton

Every cell has a cytoskeleton, which gives it shape and controls its movement. It is made up of two types of structure: **microtubules** and **microfilaments**.

Microtubules are rigid, hollow protein tubes. They are found throughout the cytoplasm, either singly or in bundles. Microtubules can be quickly put together or taken apart as they are needed by the cell. A cell structure attached to one end of a microtubule can be pushed or pulled through the cytoplasm by lengthening or shortening the microtubule. It is rather like pushing a boat out into the water by pushing against the bank with a pole. Plant cells can move chloroplasts around in this way, arranging them in the best positions to absorb sunlight.

Microfilaments are made of a different type of protein. They are solid, and much thinner than microtubules. A web-like network of microfilaments are attached to the membrane, and help give shape to the cell. They are also involved in cell movement. Some single-celled **organisms** move about by extending temporary pseudopods ("false feet"). Inside each pseudopod many hundreds of microfilaments grow rapidly in length, dragging the cell membrane along with them.

Magnified photo of cells showing the cytoskeleton. The bluish ovals are cell nuclei. The microtubules are stained red, while the microfilaments are green. Magnification approx. x 3,500.

Protein production lines

The **endoplasmic reticulum (ER)** and the **Golgi bodies** form a network of membranes within the cell called the **cytomembrane system**. This is where large molecules, in particular **lipids** and proteins, are put together.

The ER runs throughout the cytoplasm. In animal cells it is a continuation of the nuclear membrane. There are two types, rough ER and smooth ER. The outside of the rough ER is covered with tiny **ribosomes**. The ribosomes are where protein **molecules** are made, by joining together small units called **amino acids** into long chains. Ribosomes are also found on the nuclear membrane and scattered through the cytoplasm.

The ribosomes on the rough ER make proteins that are destined for use outside the cell. Many cells produce proteins for use elsewhere. For example, the cells of your pancreas (part of your digestive system) produce **enzymes** that help to digest your food. These cells have a lot of rough ER.

Smooth ER has no ribosomes and is less common than rough ER. It curves through the cytoplasm like a series of interconnected pipes. It plays a part in assembling different parts of the cell membrane.

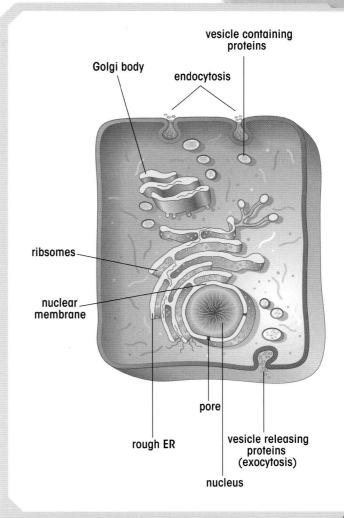

Diagram showing the cell's cytomembrane system. Proteins are assembled in the endoplasmic reticulum (ER). They then move to the Golgi body in vesicles for final changes.

Golgi bodies consist of a stack of folded membranes, rather like a pile of flattened pancakes. If the rough ER is a protein production line, then the Golgi body is the dispatcher, "addressing" the proteins to make sure that they reach the right destinations, then sending them out.

Many of the proteins will already have been labelled by the rough ER, but they may be relabelled as they pass through the Golgi body. This final sorting process is important, as it allows the proteins to link up with specific target molecules later on. The proteins are then packaged up in **vesicles** once more and sent off to their final destinations.

Plant and animal cells

Plant and animal cells, as we have seen, have some important differences. One of the most obvious differences is the plant cell wall, the rigid outer covering surrounding the cell **membrane**. The cell wall is made of fibres of **cellulose**, a type of **carbohydrate**. The rigidity of a plant cell wall places a limit on how far the cell can expand and grow.

Plant cells also have **choloroplasts**, which animal cells do not have. Choloroplasts are the cell **organelles** where the process of **photosynthesis** takes place. They are only found in the parts of plants that are exposed to the light. Many single-celled **organisms** have chloroplasts too.

Cellulose and nutrition

Although herbivores such as cows and sheep eat plants, they cannot actually produce the **enzymes** needed to break down cellulose into sugars. Instead they have to rely on colonies of bacteria living inside their guts, which do have the ability to produce this enzyme. Without their bacterial helpers, herbivores would not get the nutrition they need.

Vacuoles

Vacuoles are found in both plant and animal cells, but only plant cells have a large central vacuole. This large, membrane-bound space contains a solution of sugars and salts called sap. The central vacuole takes up most of the space in a mature plant cell; the **cytoplasm** and **nucleus** are squeezed into a thin layer between it and the cell wall.

The castor oil plant (*Fatsia japonica*) on the left is healthy and "turgid". This one on the right has lost water and consequently wilted. It is no longer in a healthy state, and cannot support itself.

The sap inside the vacuole is a more concentrated solution of chemicals than in the rest of the cell and so water tends to move into the vacuole (this is a process called **osmosis**). This causes the vacuole to expand and push the cell contents up against the inside of the cell wall. This makes the cell turgid (firm and plump). When a plant has enough water, all its cells are turgid, and this keeps the plant upright. If fluid is lost from the vacuole, the cell collapses. You can see this happening when a plant in need of watering wilts.

Cilia and flagella

Some animal cells have slender, mobile structures on the outside called **cilia** and **flagella**. They stick out from the cell membrane and are used for movement. Plant cells do not have cilia or flagella.

Flagella are long, whip-like structures that tend to occur singly. The "tails" of sperm cells are flagella. Cilia are found in large numbers and look a bit like hair. They beat together like the oars on a rowing boat. Some single-celled **organisms** are covered in a layer of tiny cilia that move them through their watery environment. Cilia are also found in various parts of the human body. For example, the cells that line the airways of your lungs are covered in cilia.

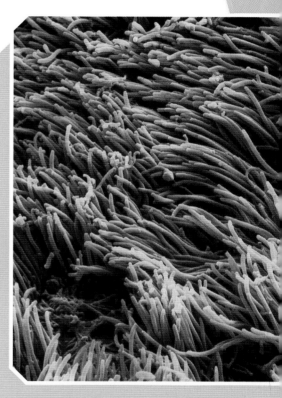

Photo taken with a scanning **electron microscope**, showing the cilia lining the air passages of the lungs. A layer of mucus traps dirt and other particles, which the cilia then sweep out of the lungs. Magnification approx. x 6,000.

Lysosomes

Lysosomes are sometimes found in plant cells but are more usually found in animal cells. These spherical bodies are separated from the rest of the cell by membranes and contain powerful digestive enzymes. Their function is to destroy worn-out organelles or to digest food particles absorbed into the cell. The digested food is then passed back through the membrane to be used by the cell.

If lysosomes break, the enzymes released into the cytoplasm digest and kill the cell. This happens when dead tissue rots, and is one of the reasons why food spoils. Lysosome enzymes are also involved in the development of a tadpole into an adult frog. As the tadpole matures, its tail slowly disappears. Lysosome enzymes are released to destroy the unwanted cells of the tail.

Light for life

All cells need raw materials (organic, carbon-containing compounds) for growth and repair. At the same time the cell needs a source of energy to carry out all this activity. The main way that living things get organic compounds and energy is through **photosynthesis**. In photosynthesis, plants take the simple **molecules** carbon dioxide (from the atmosphere) and water (from the ground), and use the energy of sunlight to build them into more complex organic compounds that provide food, not only for the plant, but also for other living things. All of the animals on the planet rely on plants as their food source, or on other animals that have eaten plants. Without plants, Earth would not be able to sustain the rich variety of life we see around us.

Catching the light

Most plants are green. But why? The colours of a plant depend on pigments within its cells. Pigments are molecules that absorb light – the colour of a pigment depends on just which wavelengths of light it absorbs and which it reflects. There are many pigments in the living world. In plants, the most important of them is a green pigment called **chlorophyll**. It is this pigment that gives green plants their colour.

Most of the chlorophyll in plant cells is found in large **organelles** called **chloroplasts**. The chloroplasts are where photosynthesis occurs. Chlorophyll plays a crucial part in photosynthesis. In the first stage of the process chlorophyll molecules, helped by other pigments, trap light energy from the Sun. This energy is used to start a chain of reactions that split water molecules into hydrogen and oxygen. This process releases chemical energy. The plant is able to "catch" this energy and store it in the bonds of a molecule called **adenosine triphosphate (ATP)**.

Chloroplasts in a plant leaf cell, shown colour enhanced. The chloroplasts are the green, oval-shaped structures around the large blue **vacuole** in the centre of the cell. The pink areas in the chloroplasts are starch grains. Magnification approx. x 4,500.

Capturing carbon

Now that the plant cells have captured energy from sunlight, they can use that energy to build new molecules.

Imagine that you are a carbon dioxide molecule drifting into the air spaces in a leaf. You find yourself beside a photosynthetic cell. Passing into the cell, you reach a chloroplast. Here, an **enzyme** called rubisco grabs hold of you and attaches you to another carbon compound. This is called carbon fixation, and it is the first step in the process that will result in the production of sugars such as **glucose**. These sugars are the building blocks for **carbohydrates** such as **cellulose** and **starch**.

Autumn accessories

Among the other pigments in green plants are the **carotenoids**. These pigments are red, orange, and yellow in colour. In most plants their colour is masked by the large quantities of chlorophyll. However, in the autumn, they become visible in the leaves of deciduous trees (trees that lose their leaves), when the chlorophyll in the leaves is broken down.

Essential waste

One product of the first stage in photosynthesis is oxygen, which is formed by the splitting of water. This "waste product" is as important to animals as the sugars and other foods that they get from plants. This is because almost all living things need oxygen for **aerobic respiration**, the most efficient way of getting energy from food.

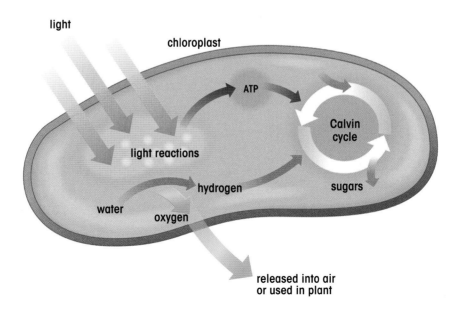

A summary of photosynthesis. During the light reaction stage, light energy is used to split water, and energy is transferred to the chemical bonds of ATP. Hydrogen, from the splitting of water, and energy from ATP are used to convert carbon dioxide into sugars.

Releasing energy

Living things need energy for all the things they do. Plants, as we have just seen, can tap into the vast source of energy from the Sun and use it to make **ATP**, the chemical energy currency of life. They then store this energy in energy-rich **molecules** such as **glucose**. Other living things get their energy by eating food – either plants, or creatures that have eaten plants. The food contains glucose and other chemicals, which can be broken down to release chemical energy. This energy is used to make ATP.

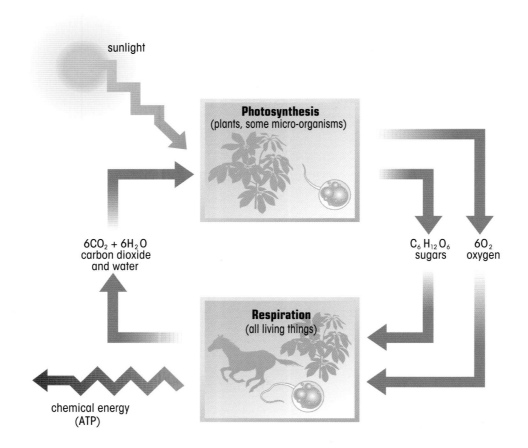

sunlight

Photosynthesis
(plants, some micro-organisms)

$6CO_2 + 6H_2O$
carbon dioxide
and water

$C_6H_{12}O_6$
sugars

$6O_2$
oxygen

Respiration
(all living things)

chemical energy
(ATP)

This diagram shows the connection between **photosynthesis** and aerobic respiration. Photosynthesis produces oxygen and stores energy in sugars. Respiration uses oxygen to release energy from sugars, producing carbon dioxide and water. Carbon dioxide and water are the raw materials for photosynthesis.

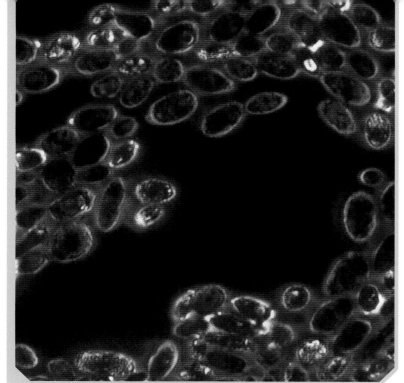

The process by which cells break down food molecules to release energy in the form of ATP is called **respiration**. In most **organisms** this process requires oxygen and is called **aerobic respiration**. Some cells (for example many bacteria) are **anaerobic**, which means they can get energy from their food without using oxygen.

A photograph taken with a light microscope showing brewer's yeast *(Saccharomyces cerevisiae)*. In the absence of oxygen, yeasts get energy by fermentation, converting sugars to ethanol (alcohol). Magnification approx. x 2,000.

Glycolysis

Whether a cell obtains its energy by aerobic or anaerobic respiration, the process begins in the same way. In the **cytoplasm** of the cell, **enzymes** split glucose molecules in a process called **glycolysis**. The initial steps of this reaction actually require energy, and use up two ATP molecules. However, in the course of the reaction four new ATP molecules are formed, so there is a net gain of two ATP per glucose molecule.

Anaerobic respiration

A wide variety of living things make use of anaerobic respiration. Examples are bacteria and other single-celled organisms that live in places where there is little oxygen (such as marshes, stagnant ponds, and inside the guts of animals). The bacteria used to make yoghurt and the yeasts used to make bread all use anaerobic respiration.

Organisms that use anaerobic respiration get energy from glycolysis, but then go a step further to form end products. One such end product, lactate, is sometimes referred to as **lactic acid**. This is the process used by the bacteria that produce cheese and yoghurt. Lactate is also formed in your muscle cells when they have to produce energy quickly.

Another kind of anaerobic respiration has ethanol (alcohol) as the end product. Yeasts, which we use in bread-making, brewing beer, and making wine, use this pathway. Wild yeast cells live on grapes and other fruits and berries. Birds sometimes get drunk by feasting on naturally **fermenting** berries!

Powerhouses of the cell

Most cells obtain their energy by **aerobic respiration**. This process requires oxygen, and breaks down sugars to carbon dioxide and water.

If there is oxygen available, aerobic respiration can happen. The products of **glycolysis** pass out of the **cytoplasm** into the **mitochondria**. These rod-like or spherical **organelles** are often called the powerhouses of the cell. All cells except bacteria and **archaea** have mitochondria in their cytoplasm. They are a vital part of living cells, supplying most of the cell's energy needs. The more active a cell is, the more mitochondria it has. Some cells, such as human liver cells, contain more than 1,000 mitochondria.

Inside mitochondria, the products of glycolysis are combined with oxygen and broken down into water and carbon dioxide. The process involves a complex chain of chemical reactions called the **Krebs cycle**, or citric acid cycle, and it releases large amounts of energy. Aerobic respiration is much more efficient than **anaerobic respiration**. Overall, 32 **ATP molecules** can be produced from a single molecule of **glucose**, 16 times more than the 2 ATP molecules produced by glycolysis alone.

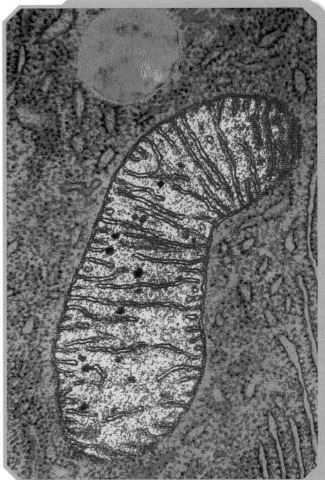

A false-colour photograph taken with an **electron microscope** showing a mitochondrion. The membrane folds, or cristae, where respiration takes place can be seen within the mitochondrion. Magnification approx. x 20,000.

The mitochondrial membrane

The **membrane** around a mitochondrion is a double one. The outer membrane is smooth, but the inner membrane has many folds, called **cristae**. The cristae are lined by tiny structures that contain the **enzymes** that break down chemicals and generate ATP. In cells that have high energy needs, the mitochondria have more cristae and thus more enzyme-containing structures.

Mitochondria and bacteria

Bacteria, unlike most other living cells, have no mitochondria. A typical bacterium, in fact, is very much like a free-living mitochondrion. Most scientists now believe that mitochondria evolved from bacteria. At a very early stage in the history of life these bacteria began to live inside larger cells, and eventually became a part of them.

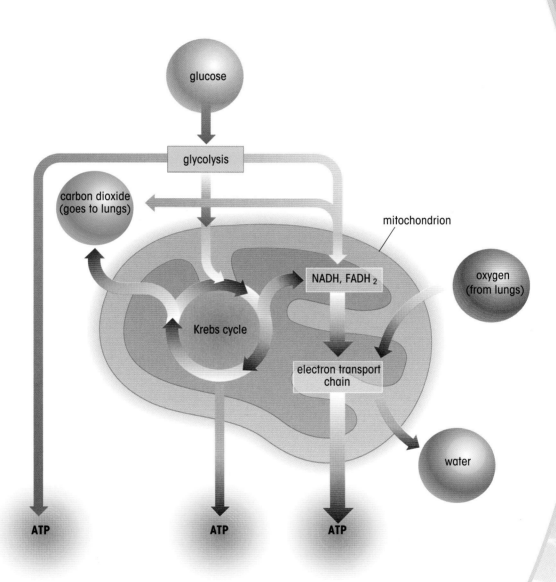

An overview of respiration. NADH and $FADH_2$ are molecules that store energy in a similar way to ATP. In a process called **electron** transport phosphorylation, the energy from NADH and $FADH_2$ is converted to ATP.

Protein production

Probably the most complex and important of the large **molecules** in a cell are the **proteins**. All the structures of a cell are built mostly from proteins. A special class of proteins, called **enzymes**, controls the enormous range of chemical reactions that go on inside living cells.

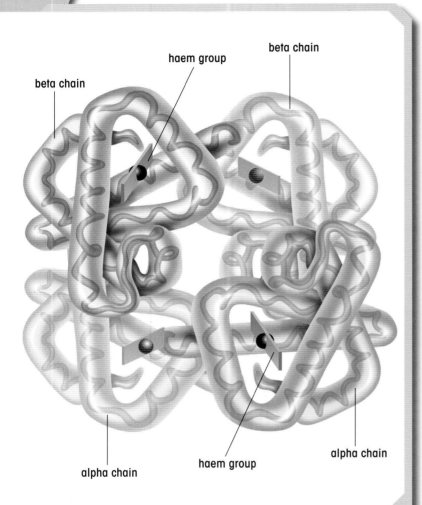

beta chain

haem group

beta chain

beta chain

alpha chain

haem group

alpha chain

Once a protein chain has formed, it may team up with other protein chains to form a complex protein. This illustration shows haemoglobin, a protein found in red blood cells. It is made up of four protein chains and four small molecules called haem groups.

Without enzymes there would be no life. A cell needs thousands of enzymes to perform its essential tasks, such as obtaining energy, moving, growing, and repairing itself. Each reaction that takes place in the cell has its own specific enzyme. Because the enzymes control the reactions, they effectively control the cell.

Protein assembly

Proteins are complex, three-dimensional substances made of chains of smaller molecules called **amino acids**. There are twenty kinds of amino acid commonly used in protein building. Each protein has a very specific structure, with a certain number of amino acids in a particular order. So how does the cell ensure that the correct number of amino acids are linked in the right order to make a particular protein?

DNA

The instruction book for assembling proteins in the cell is contained within the structure of another remarkable molecule – **DNA (deoxyribonucleic acid)**.

Like proteins, DNA molecules are made up of many smaller units. Each of these is one letter in a code that can be "read" by the cell. This code is called the genetic code, because it comes in segments called genes. Each gene is the template for building a protein or part of a protein.

Every living thing has a unique form of DNA. All forms of life, from the simplest single-celled bacterium to the cells of all plants and animals, contain at least one DNA molecule. Whenever a cell divides, it first makes a copy of its DNA, so that each new cell has its own protein instruction kit.

Following the instructions

The **nucleus** is the largest and most conspicuous **organelle** in the cells of **eukaryotes**. This is where the cell's DNA is found. Bacteria have no nucleus, but they still have DNA in their **cytoplasm**. The DNA molecules are folded and coiled up to form structures called **chromosomes**. Just before a cell divides, the chromosomes coil even more, and become visible.

In many cells a dark, oval area called the **nucleolus** can be seen within the nucleus. Here, parts of the chromosomes are unwound so that the protein assembly instructions can be read. Molecules of a substance called **messenger RNA**, which is similar to DNA, copy the instructions and carry them from the nucleus into the cytoplasm.

The messenger RNA then goes to the **ribosomes**, where the proteins will be assembled. A ribosome moves along the messenger RNA, following the instructions it carries. Amino acids are brought to the messenger RNA and linked together in the right order to form the protein.

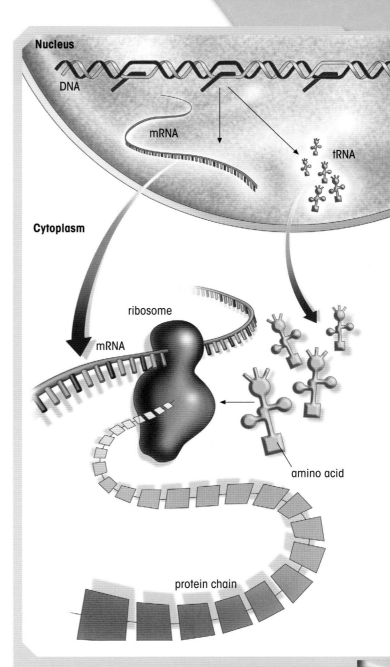

An overview of protein synthesis. The instructions for making a protein are copied from DNA, then carried from the nucleus to the cytoplasm by messenger RNA (mRNA). The mRNA feeds through the ribosome, which reads the instructions, joining together amino acids in the order specified. Another molecule, transfer RNA (tRNA) is responsible for bringing amino acids to the ribosome.

3

Protistans

More than 200,000 **protistan** species have been named and described, and there are probably millions more. Most are single-celled **organisms** and all are **eukaryotes**, which distinguishes them from the bacteria and **archaea**. They are sometimes divided into three main groups, though this does not do justice to the diversity of the protistans:

- fungus-like protistans, such as water moulds and slime moulds
- animal-like protistans, often known as the **protozoans** (meaning "first animals")
- plant-like protistans, which include the **algae**.

Protistans come in a wide variety of forms. Some have scales, shells, and highly elaborate skeletons. Some even form multi-cellular colonies. The colonies of some marine protistans can be made up of hundreds of cells encased within a long tube that may be more than a metre long. In contrast, some protistan **parasites** are small enough to invade the cells of other organisms.

Protistans are found practically everywhere. They have adapted to life across a range of habitats from the polar oceans to the tropical rainforests, from the ocean floor to the summits of mountains. Even your body is a thriving habitat for protistans.

Plant-like protistans

The protistans that are capable of **photosynthesis** are often informally grouped together as members of the algae. This is a loose grouping that also includes some multi-cellular organisms such as the red, green, and brown seaweeds. Some seaweeds can be as big as trees. Most algae live in water, although a few live in damp places on land, such as the surface of moist soil, damp rocks, and tree trunks. The majority are classed as **phytoplankton**. These are single-celled, water-living creatures that are the basic food of all animals in the oceans, rivers, and lakes.

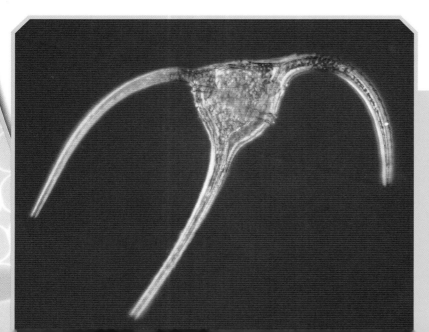

The dinoflagellate *Ceratium tripos*. Dinoflagellates are single-celled protistans, usually found in the oceans. They can either feed like animals, or photosynthesize, like plants. Magnification approx. x 1,250.

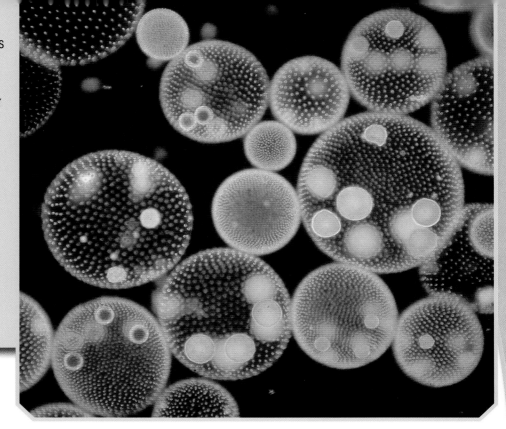

Whirling colonies of the protistan *Volvox*. The individual *Volvox* cells each have a whip-like flagellum. Each colony is a hollow ball of between 500 and 10,000 individuals. Magnification approx. x 30.

- The green algae include about 17,000 species, ranging from *Chlorella* (a simple alga, consisting of a single spherical cell containing one large **chloroplast**) to large seaweeds such as sea lettuce. Green algae are thought to be closely related to true plants because they have **cellulose** cell walls, use the same types of **chlorophyll**, and store food in the form of **starch**. The chlorophyll gives them a bright green colour. Although **flagella** are characteristic of animal cells, some single-celled species of green alga are able to swim about using flagella.

- The chrysophytes are mostly free-living photosynthesizers. The golden and yellow-green algae included in this group get their colour from photosynthetic pigments called **carotenoids**. Most chrysophytes live in fresh water.

- Euglenoids are single-celled organisms that are difficult to classify as they have some animal and some plant-like characteristics. They can move around using a flagellum, a characteristic of animal cells. Most of them have chloroplasts, a characteristic of plant cells, but some do not. Unlike green algae they do not store food as starch, and they lack rigid cellulose cell walls, having a **protein** coat called a pellicle instead. There are around 1,000 species.

- Diatoms are common in marine and freshwater habitats. They have intricate, jewel-like shells formed from two perforated parts that overlap like the lid on a box.

- The 2,000 or so species of dinoflagellate typically have two flagella for getting around and an outer protective coat formed from plates of cellulose. This coat varies enormously in shape between species. Dinoflagellates live in both fresh water and seawater.

Protozoans

The animal-like **protistans** can be known collectively as **protozoans** ("first animals"). Protozoa are found everywhere there is moisture, including ocean and freshwater environments, in damp soil, and inside the moist interior of other **organisms**.

Protozoans are unable to make their own food and must find and consume it. They move actively through their environment in search of nutrition; some are grazers, others **predators**, and some are **parasites**. Here are some examples.

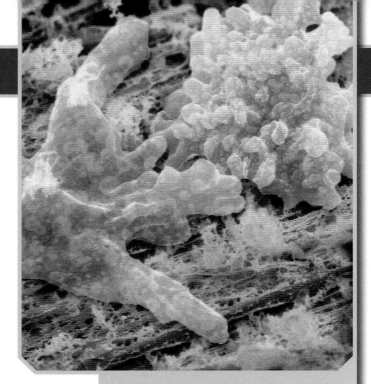

The *Amoeba* proteus putting out pseudopodia to engulf another amoeba of the same species. Magnification approx. x 150.

Amoeba-like protozoans

These protozoans are very common everywhere in soil and water. They move around by forming pseudopods ('false feet'), temporary extensions of the cell formed by **microfilaments**. Most feed by completely surrounding their prey, which can be either smaller protozoans or **algae**, and engulfing it (phagocytosis). The food item ends up enclosed inside the cell in a **vacuole**, into which digestive **enzymes** are secreted. The digested prey then passes back into the **cytoplasm**, and any undigestable material is expelled from the cell.

Foraminifera and radiolaria

These groups of protozoa have hard, protective shells through which long, thread-like pseudopodia extend. These act as sticky traps to catch other micro-organisms.

Ciliophora

The ciliophora, or ciliated protozoans, have numerous tiny **cilia** on their surface. Most ciliates use these to swim through their watery environments where they prey on bacteria, algae, and each other. The cilia beat in waves, propelling the organism along, and also wafting food particles into the cell. Ciliates are unusual in possessing two types of **nucleus**. The larger macronucleus controls the cell's **metabolism**, while the smaller micronucleus is involved only in reproduction.

The ciliates come in a variety of shapes. *Vorticella*, for example, is a group of bell-shaped cells that attach themselves to a surface (such as the leaf of an aquatic plant) by a long, stalk-like extension. *Paramecium* on the other hand is a streamlined, oval cell that is completely covered with cilia. It shoots out tiny poisonous threads called trichocysts when it is irritated.

Sporozoans

Sporozoans are parasitic protistans that complete part of their life cycle inside other cells. At one end of the cell body there is a cluster of distinctive **organelles** that are used in penetrating host cells. The life cycle is often complex, involving several different host species.

Malaria – a sporozoan disease

The best-known example of a sporozoan is *Plasmodium*, which causes malaria. *Plasmodium* gets into humans through the bite of an infected female mosquito. **Spore**-like infective cells called sporozoites are introduced into the victim's blood. These cells reproduce first in the liver and then in red blood cells. Some of the sporozoites grow and produce sex cells while in the blood, and these are picked up if the infected person is bitten again by a mosquito. Inside the mosquito's digestive tract hundreds of new sporozoite cells are formed, and these travel to the mosquito's salivary glands, ready to infect the next person it bites.

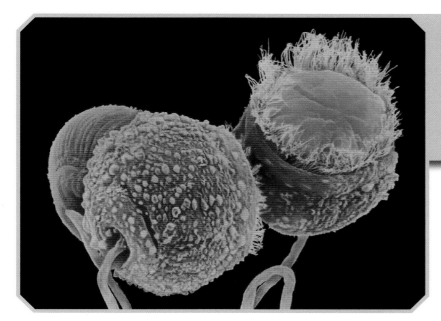

Scanning electron micrograph of *Vorticella* cells. The top of each one has a ring of cilia that beat bacteria and other organisms into the *Vorticella*. Magnification approx. x 1,200.

4

The prokaryotes: bacteria

Once regarded as a single kingdom, the **prokaryotes** are now split into two – the bacteria and the **archaea**. One prokaryote can be as distinct from another as a kangaroo is from a flea. Of all living **organisms**, prokaryotes are the most widespread. They are found practically everywhere on Earth, including places where other organisms could not survive. Some thrive at temperatures of 110 °C (230 °F) or more; others live in acid soils and waters, in extremely salty environments, or under the high-pressure and freezing conditions at the bottom of the ocean. Prokaryotes have been found living over 2,500 metres (8,202 feet) below the Earth's surface and in the air more than 8 kilometres (5 miles) above it. They are in the soil, in water droplets and in dust particles in the air, and inside the digestive systems of all animals in their countless billions. The prokaryotes you carry around outnumber the cells that make up your body by ten to one.

Types of bacteria

Bacteria are grouped into three basic categories according to their shape:

- the cocci, roughly spherical in form
- the bacilli, rod-shaped or cylindrical in form with rounded ends
- the spirilla, rigid, spiral or coiled rods.

Scanning electron micrograph showing bacteria (yellow and green) on the surface of a human tooth. Magnification approx. x 5,300.

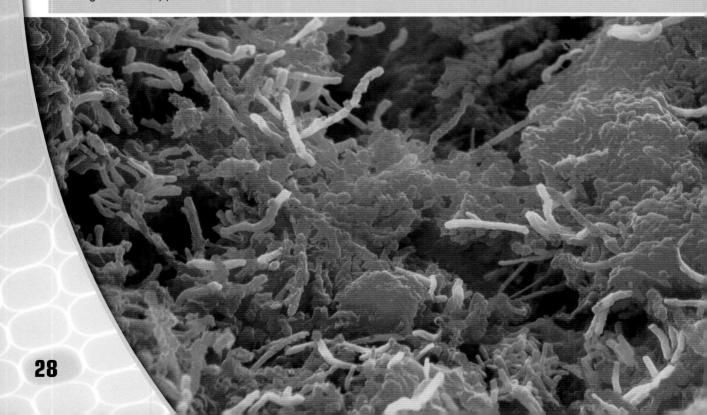

However, this is something of a simplification, as some cocci can be oval or flattened, bacilli can be long and thin like straws, and some bacteria found in salty ponds are square-shaped. Bacteria are much smaller than the cells that make up multi-cellular organisms such as plants and animals. The average bacterium is about a tenth of the size of an average plant or animal cell.

Bacteria on the outside

Bacterial cells are usually surrounded by a protective cell wall. Many types of bacteria can be identified by their cell walls. Doctors use a common laboratory test of this type to identify which kind of bacteria is causing an infection. This helps them decide which **antibiotics** would be most effective against the infection.

Around the cell wall there may be a sticky mesh, forming a capsule or slime layer around the bacterium. This helps the bacterium to attach itself to surfaces like rocks or teeth. The mesh also gives the bacterium an added layer of protection.

Bacteria on the inside

The **DNA** of a bacterium is contained in a single, circular **chromosome** and in smaller circular structures called **plasmids**. A bacterium has no large internal structures such as **chloroplasts** or **mitochondria**. Few bacteria have any internal divisions at all and all their **metabolic** processes are carried out in the **cytoplasm** or on the **cell membrane**. However, there are **ribosomes** for **protein** production scattered throughout the cytoplasm, or attached to the inside of the **plasma membrane**.

This illustration shows the structure of a typical rod-shaped bacterium.

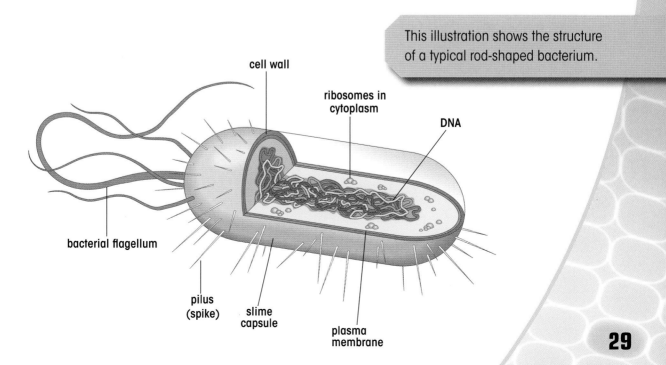

cell wall

ribosomes in cytoplasm

DNA

bacterial flagellum

pilus (spike)

slime capsule

plasma membrane

Archaea: life at the extreme

Until recently it was believed that life could be split neatly into two groups, or kingdoms: the **prokaryotes**, which have no nucleus in their cells, and the **eukaryotes**, which do. Then in 1977 Carl R. Woese of the University of Illinois discovered that a group of micro-organisms that had until then been classified as bacteria were actually different enough to be given their own kingdom in the living world. This has led to a division of the prokaryotes into two distinct kingdoms: the **archaea** and the bacteria. It has even been suggested that the archaea are so different they should be in their own domain of life.

Early life

Many of the archaea and some bacteria are adapted to the conditions widely believed to have existed on the early Earth, i.e. great heat and little or no oxygen. For this reason most scientists suspect that the two groups diverged from a common ancestor relatively soon after life began.

The archaea are similar to the bacteria in many ways. They too lack a **nucleus**, for example. However, archaea have some genes that are found in eukaryotes rather than prokaryotes. More importantly, over half the genes of an archaea are completely different from the genes in any other **organism**. These unshared genes may offer valuable clues to the origin and evolution of life on Earth.

The gut of a cow is home to many archaea.

The great Salt Lake in Utah, USA is both very salty and alkaline (the opposite of acidic). Some archaea can live even in this extreme environment.

Extremophiles

Most archaea are tough creatures found in some of the Earth's most extreme environments, for example near volcanic vents or in salt concentrations that would kill other organisms. For this reason they are also known as **extremophiles**.

Some of the best-known of the extremophiles are the deep-sea bacteria such as *Pyrococcus furiosus* (the "Flaming Fireball"). They are found near volcanic vents 3,000 metres (9,842 feet) below the ocean surface. Superheated lava oozes out of these vents at temperatures up to 400 °C (752 °F). Bacteria such as *Pyrococcus* are found living near these vents, at temperatures of around 100 °C (212 °F).

Another group of archaea, the halophiles, live in extremely salty environments, such as salt lakes and evaporation ponds where salt is collected. An ordinary cell suspended in a very salty solution will quickly lose water and become dehydrated, because water tends to flow from areas of low salt concentration to areas of higher concentration. Halophiles deal with this problem by having high concentrations of salt within the cell. One archaean, known as *Halobacterium salinarum*, concentrates potassium chloride in its interior.

Perhaps the grimmest of all the environments where extremophiles are found is hot, concentrated sulphuric acid. Some bacteria that live in hot volcanic springs, such as the geysers in Yellowstone National Park, USA, use sulphur as a source of energy and produce sulphuric acid as a waste product. These bacteria thrive in strong sulphuric acid at 85 °C (185 °F).

If there is life elsewhere in the Solar System, buried deep in Martian rocks or hidden beneath the ice in the oceans of Jupiter's moon Europa, it may well resemble the extremophiles.

Prokaryote behaviour

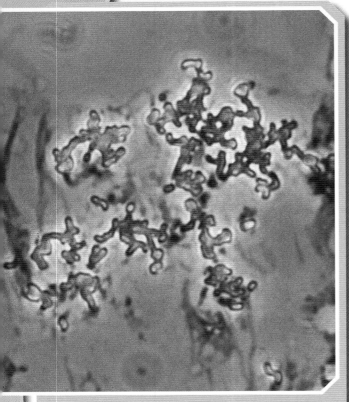

These bacteria (*Thiobacillus thioparvus*) need sulphur in their diet. They can sense substances containing sulphur and move towards them to feed. Magnification approx. x 800.

Many **prokaryotes** have chemical receptors that allow them to detect changes in the concentration of chemicals such as sugars, oxygen, and carbon dioxide in their surroundings. They can also sense changes in temperature, and **photosynthetic** bacteria respond to changes in light. A few bacteria can sense the direction of a magnetic field. These magnetotactic bacteria have a chain of tiny particles of a magnetic material called magnetite inside their cells. This acts like a tiny compass. In water they use this ability to swim along magnetic lines of force to reach their preferred environment.

While swimming, prokaryotes are constantly monitoring the concentration of chemicals in their environment. The concentrations of these chemicals can affect the direction in which the **organisms** move. Millions of *Myxococcus xanthus* bacteria will change direction together to move towards a possible food source, such as other bacteria. The "prey" bacteria get stuck to the *Myxococcus* colony, which produces **enzymes** to digest them.

Magnetotactic Martians

In the year 2000, an international team of researchers discovered long chains of magnetite crystals embedded in a meteorite that reached Earth from Mars. The magnetite crystals are similar to those formed by magnetotactic bacteria on Earth. Some scientists believe these chains could only have been formed by once-living organisms. "Such a chain of magnets outside an organism would immediately collapse into a clump due to magnetic forces," said Dr Imre Friedmann, of NASA's Ames Research Center.

Growth and reproduction

Prokaryotes live their lives at a far faster rate than **eukaryote** cells. Some of their enzyme systems operate very quickly indeed. Whereas it might take a cell in your body some minutes to assemble a **protein molecule**, a prokaryote can do it in seconds. Under the most favourable conditions some prokaryotes can reproduce and double in number every 20 minutes or so. Under natural conditions, however, limited food supplies mean that they only divide every few days.

Prokaryote cell division occurs by binary fission (splitting in two). The two resulting cells may separate from each other, or remain attached to form a chain, or filament, of cells.

If conditions are unfavourable, some bacteria form a thick-walled structure called an endospore around their **DNA** and some of their **cytoplasm**. The endospore is resistant to heat, drying, radiation, boiling, and disinfectants. Endospores can remain dormant for many years until conditions improve. The endospore then becomes active once again, developing into a new bacterium.

Getting around

Many prokaryotes have no means of moving themselves and simply float aimlessly in the water, or on the wind, or are carried around on animals they have infected. Others, however, can move about by means of tiny hair-like **flagella**. These hollow, rod-like structures are formed from long strands of protein that project through the organism's cell wall. They are much simpler in structure than the flagella of eukaryote cells. The flagellum rotates like a propeller, moving the organism along.

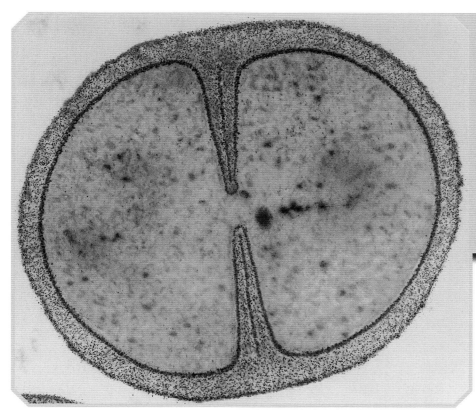

A *Staphylococcus epidermidis* bacterium in the process of dividing. Under optimum conditions, a single bacterium could in theory form a colony of billions within a single day. Magnification approx. x 130,000.

Prokaryote metabolism

Prokaryotes may be extremely small, with little in the way of internal structure, but this does not mean that they are simple. They have a greater variety of ways of obtaining energy than **eukaryote** cells. Like the eukaryotes, prokaryotes can be divided into self-feeders, or autotrophs (**organisms** like green plants that can manufacture their food from simple raw materials) and other feeders, or heterotrophs (organisms like humans and other animals that have to eat other organisms to get food). Autotrophs use carbon dioxide from the air as their major source of carbon, linking it with other chemicals to manufacture the materials they need. Heterotrophs consume carbon compounds that have been produced by other organisms. Most prokaryotes are heterotrophs.

Self-feeding prokaryotes

Some autotrophic bacteria use energy from sunlight to make sugars from carbon dioxide and water, just as plants do. Many of them use a type of **chlorophyll** to capture the Sun's energy. The blue-green bacteria, or cyanobacteria, make sugars in this way.

Archaea that live in very high salt concentrations, such as the Dead Sea, are able to turn light energy into chemical energy. They use the light energy to manufacture **ATP**. This process is quite different from plant **photosynthesis**.

Many prokaryotes can obtain energy from chemicals instead of from light. They use this energy to produce the food they need. This process is called **chemosynthesis** ("made with chemical energy") rather than photosynthesis ("made with light energy").

The archaea that live around volcanic vents deep in the sea are chemosynthetic. They make food and get energy from hydrogen sulphide and other chemicals that pour out of the vents.

Salmonella are bacteria that move around using **flagella**. They live in the digestive systems of many types of mammal. Some kinds of *Salmonella* cause diseases in humans, such as salmonellosis and typhoid. Magnification approx. x 11,000.

Prokaryotes that feed on others

Most prokaryotes get their food ready made. They feed on a wide range of materials, including both living and dead plant and animal material. Those prokaryotes that feed on dead material are a vital part of the living world. They act as decomposers and recyclers, making raw materials available for reuse by the food producers. Bacteria that feed on living organisms are generally **parasites**, and often cause disease. No archaea are known to cause disease.

Prokaryotes digest their food by producing **enzymes** that break down the food before it is absorbed into the cell. The digested food is then absorbed into the organism. When a piece of food goes bad and turns mushy, it is often because it is being broken down by millions of bacteria.

The green surface of this puddle is produced by cyanobacteria. Cyanobacteria are plant-like bacteria that make their own food by photosynthesis. The ancestors of today's cyanobacteria were probably the first living things on Earth to photosynthesize.

Respiration

Most prokaryotes are **aerobic**; they need oxygen for **respiration**, just as we do. But some prokaryotes are **anaerobic**, which means they do not need oxygen. For an anaerobic prokaryote, oxygen may in fact be a poison. Some anaerobic bacteria get energy by **fermenting** sugar. They can be very useful to us as they produce **lactic acid**. They are used in the production of butter and yoghurt. Other bacteria convert alcohol into acetic acid and are used to make vinegar. Still others produce methane gas, a valuable fuel that is becoming more widespread as an energy source.

5

Viruses: out on the border

Viruses are simple but effective disease agents. Viruses have been found in plants, insects, mammals, fish, **protistans**, bacteria, and **archaea**. There are no cell types that are immune from virus attack. Viruses themselves are not complete living **organisms**. They lie on the border between the living and non-living worlds. They are true **parasites**, depending entirely on a living organism, called a host, for their needs.

Essentially a virus is a set of instructions for making a new virus (a **DNA** or **RNA molecule** wrapped up in a protective coat). The virus cannot "read" these instructions by itself. Viruses lack the **enzymes** and other chemicals necessary for reproduction. The only way they can reproduce is by entering a living cell and taking over its biochemical processes to manufacture new viruses. The damage caused to cells by the assembly of the new viruses is what produces the symptoms of viral disease.

There may only be enough genetic material in a small virus for three or four genes, while larger viruses will have around a hundred genes. Compare this to the 20,000–25,000 genes in humans.

Viruses range in size from 20 to 200 millionths of a millimetre. The full stop at the end of this sentence is around half a millimetre across – that is big enough to hold about 5,000 medium-sized viruses.

Although the existence of viruses was suspected by the end of the 19th century, it was not until the **electron microscope** was perfected in the years after the Second World War that scientists first saw what a virus looked like. Viruses come in a variety of shapes and cause a wide variety of diseases – AIDS, rabies, polio, measles, influenza, and the common cold are just a few examples.

Diagram of a "typical" virus. Simple viruses consist of a strand of either DNA or RNA surrounded by a coat of protein, or protein and **lipid**. Some viruses are more complex, with a **membrane** around the DNA or RNA, and perhaps tail fibres and other structures.

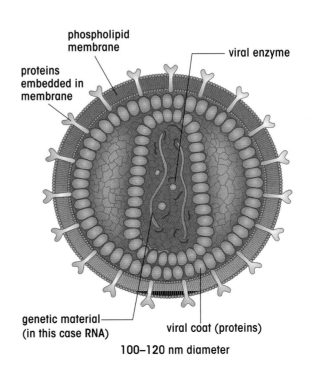

phospholipid membrane

viral enzyme

proteins embedded in membrane

genetic material (in this case RNA)

viral coat (proteins)

100–120 nm diameter

Mounting a defence

The human body has several lines of defence against virus attacks. First, if a particular virus infects some of the cells in your body, the infected cells make a type of **protein** called interferon. Interferon works with the cells surrounding the infected cells, helping them to become more resistant to the virus. Sometimes this works, but sometimes it doesn't. If the resistance is not strong enough, the virus continues to spread and affect more and more cells.

Another line of defence is the body's immune system. It acts by killing infected cells. Killing infected cells is a bit like making a firebreak to stop a forest fire spreading. A virus needs a living cell in order to reproduce itself. By killing infected cells the immune system takes away the virus's "fuel". Eventually, if the immune system does its job, the virus will run out of places to make new viruses.

Antibodies are the body's most effective defence against viruses. Antibodies are proteins produced by the immune system. They bind with the virus, making it harmless or destroying it altogether. The body makes large amounts of antibodies when a virus invader is detected. However, antibodies have no effect against viruses inside cells.

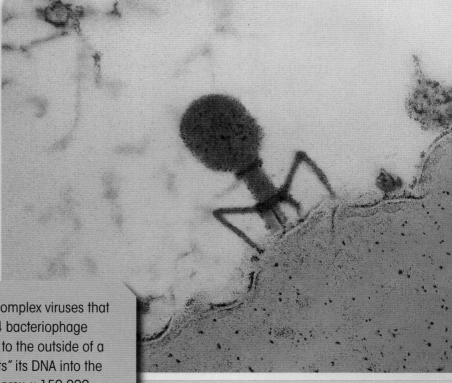

Where did they come from?

No one knows how viruses first emerged. They may have originated as pieces of genetic material that escaped from cells and gained the ability to reproduce themselves by passing from one cell to another.

Bacteriophages are complex viruses that infect bacteria. The T4 bacteriophage shown here attaches to the outside of a bacterium and "injects" its DNA into the cell. Magnification approx. x 150,000.

6

Under the microscope

We have seen that cells are very small – too small to be seen with the unaided eye. Until the invention of the **microscope**, no one had any idea that cells existed at all.

The compound microscope

In a modern compound light microscope two or more lenses bend light reflected from the object being examined to form an enlarged image of it. Compound microscopes are widely used in biology and medicine to study bacteria and other single-celled **organisms**, and plant and animal cells. Compound microscopes have a maximum magnification of about 1,000 to 1,500 times. They can show structures in the cell such as the **nucleus**, **chloroplasts**, and **mitochondria**.

Biologists use a variety of techniques when studying cells with a compound microscope. They can take very thin sections of cells using an instrument called a microtome, and use dyes to pick out various cell structures.

The unaided eye can distinguish objects about half a millimetre apart. A light microscope can separate objects less than a micrometre apart, but an electron microscope can distinguish objects down to almost 0.1 nanometres (billionths of a metre).

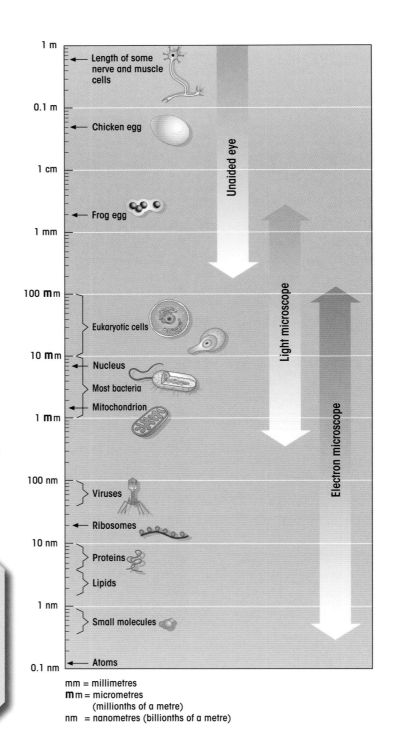

1 m — Length of some nerve and muscle cells

0.1 m — Chicken egg

1 cm

Frog egg

1 mm

Unaided eye

100 **m**m — Eukaryotic cells

Light microscope

10 **m**m — Nucleus

Most bacteria

Electron microscope

1 **m**m — Mitochondrion

100 nm — Viruses

Ribosomes

10 nm — Proteins

Lipids

1 nm — Small molecules

0.1 nm — Atoms

mm = millimetres
mm = micrometres
(millionths of a metre)
nm = nanometres (billionths of a metre)

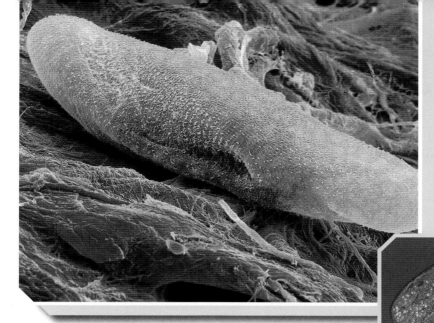

Two images of the protistan *Paramecium*. The image below is from a light microscope, while the image on the left is from a scanning electron microscope. The light microscope image shows details from inside the cell, but it is two-dimensional. Magnifications approx. x 640 (below) and x 800 (left).

Van Leeuwenhoek

In the last half of the 17th century, a Dutch businessman called Antonie van Leeuwenhoek made hand-polished lenses that could magnify an incredible 300 times. With his simple, single-lens microscopes he became the first person to observe living cells, including blood cells and single-celled organisms in pond water. His lenses were so good that he was almost certainly also the first person to see bacteria.

Digital video microscopy makes use of advances in digital video cameras and computer enhancement to observe living cells. Using this technique biologists can study small transparent objects that would otherwise be almost impossible to see.

The electron microscope

Instead of lenses and light rays, the **electron microscope** uses electromagnetic fields to focus a stream of subatomic particles called **electrons** on to an object. The image appears on a fluorescent screen, similar to a television. An electron microscope can give 100 times greater magnification than a light microscope. It reveals more of the detailed structure of the cell.

There are two basic types of electron microscope. The transmission electron microscope projects a beam of electrons through the specimen being observed. Samples to be studied using a transmission electron microscope have to be very thin indeed.

The scanning electron microscope sends a narrow beam of electrons back and forth across a specimen that has had a very thin coat of metal applied to it. The metal gives off electrons, which are picked up by a detector to produce an image of the specimen on a television screen. The scanning electron microscope produces images of fantastic depth and clarity.

The electron microscope allows scientists to examine the detailed structure of **organelles** such as the mitochondria, and reveals structures such as **ribosomes**, which are too small to be seen with a light microscope. Scientists can also see **viruses**, which are smaller than the smallest bacterium.

7

First cells

Cells are made of a complex soup of chemicals, all reacting together in a controlled way to produce what we call life. Cells assemble all the **molecules** they need, such as **proteins**, **carbohydrates**, and **nucleic acids**, using simpler compounds and energy that they obtain from their environment. The result of all this complex chemical interaction is movement, feeding, reproduction, and all the other characteristics of life. But how did this all come about?

As far as we know, Earth spent the first 500 million years of its existence being hit by huge meteorites, pieces of rock left over from the formation of the Solar System. Some of these collisions were so ferocious that the oceans boiled and turned to gas. At least one impact was powerful enough to knock off a chunk of the Earth (this chunk became the Moon). The young Sun was weaker than it is now and even after the worst of the bombardment was over, the Earth was gripped by planet-wide ice ages.

Despite the harshness of the conditions, somehow, probably during the first billion years of Earth's history, complex molecules began forming and reproducing themselves. They got their energy from chemicals or from sunlight. All the chemicals needed to form organic molecules were present on the early Earth and perhaps lightning, energy from the Sun, or heat from inside the Earth provided the energy to form more complex molecules.

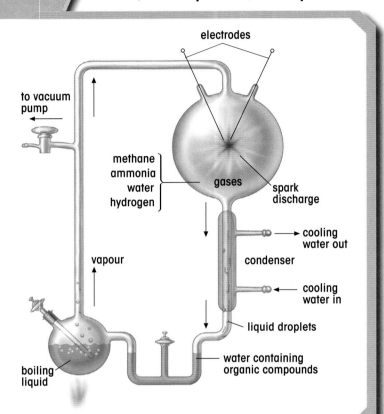

This diagram shows the apparatus Miller and Urey used to simulate the conditions in which we think early life arose.

Life modelling

In 1953 Harold Urey and Stanley Miller carried out an experiment to show that it was possible to produce organic molecules under conditions believed to resemble those found on Earth billions of years ago. They mixed methane, hydrogen, ammonia, and water inside a reaction chamber and then bombarded the mixture with electrical discharges to simulate lightning. In less than a week, **amino acids** and other organic compounds had formed.

Shaping life from clay?

Urey and Miller's experiment showed that it was possible to form simple organic compounds, but how did more complex molecules form? One theory is that flat beds of clay, washed by the tides, were sites for the assembly of **proteins** and other compounds. Clay is formed of thin stacked layers of material with ions (charged particles) that attract amino acids at their surfaces. If you expose amino acids to clay, warm the clay in the sun, and alternately moisten and dry it (as would happen with the rise and fall of tides) reactions take place that produce proteins and other compounds.

Another idea is that organic compounds formed near hydrothermal vents, places where hot volcanic lava bursts out from under the Earth on to the ocean floor. These are the sort of places where **archaea** are found today. Experiments have shown that when amino acids are heated and placed in water they form small protein-like molecules called proteinoids.

Chemical competition

If some of the proteins formed by whatever means acted as **enzymes**, promoting the formation of other proteins, an evolutionary "protein competition" could have got under way. The next step might have been the emergence of **metabolism** – the harnessing of energy to bring about chemical reactions. Metabolism is a key characteristic of life.

If organic compounds such as enzymes and **ATP** formed in the same location, they would begin to react together chemically and so, over time, the pattern of reactions found in cell metabolism today could begin to emerge.

Another characteristic of living things is their ability to reproduce. To do this they must make copies of **DNA** molecules, the chemical instruction manuals for making proteins. Quite how DNA first emerged we do not yet know.

A hydrothermal vent in the Pacific Ocean. Giant tubeworms and tiny white crabs are among the creatures that thrive around such vents.

Building cells

The proteinoids mentioned on the previous pages were found to form small stable spheres after cooling. Could a similar process have led to the formation of the first cell **membranes**? Like cell membranes, proteinoid spheres are selectively permeable, allowing some substances in and out but not others. Other experiments have produced membrane-like sacs from **lipids** (fats). Such spheres forming around **proteins**, **ATP**, and other chemicals would protect and isolate them from the environment, perhaps allowing the development of **metabolic** processes.

Earliest life

The first identifiable living cells appeared perhaps 3.9 billion years ago. How and where this happened we will never know. We believe that they were similar to today's bacteria. They were **prokaryote** cells, in other words, lacking a **nucleus**. Possibly they were little different from the lipid spheres described above. They had plenty of time to develop: food was abundant, energy plentiful, and there were no **predators**.

At some point the family line diverged, one branch becoming the bacteria and the other giving rise to the **archaea** and eventually the **eukaryotes**, which would one day lead to the huge variety of multi-cellular life that includes us.

Between 3.5 and 3.2 billion years ago the first **photosynthesizers** appeared. This was a major step in the development of life. Photosynthesis not only made the vast source of energy from the Sun available to Earth's developing lifeforms, it also released oxygen into the atmosphere. This had a profound effect. Oxygen is a very active chemical and prevents complex organic compounds from forming. So the cells that populated the Earth at that time had to adapt to the new oxygen-rich atmosphere, or take up homes in places where oxygen was scarce.

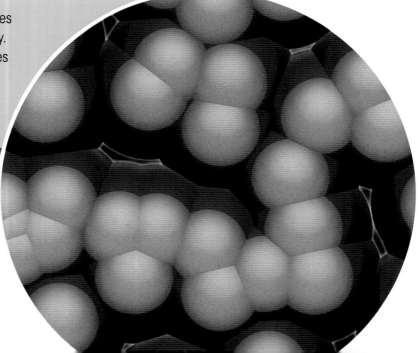

These protein and lipid spheres were created in the laboratory. They have the same properties as the cell membranes found in living organisms. Magnification approx. x 400.

Another consequence of the rising oxygen levels was that the conditions under which life originally emerged were now gone for good. Life would not be able to start from scratch again because the delicate molecules involved would be disrupted by the reactive oxygen.

Endosymbiosis

Eukaryotic cells, the sort that make up our bodies, may have come about by a series of happy accidents. According to one theory, eukaryotes appeared as a result of endosymbiosis. Endo- means "within" and symbiosis means "living together". Around 1.2 billion years ago the ancestors of the eukaryotes may have been something like **amoebae** that engulfed aerobic bacteria. Perhaps some of these bacteria resisted being digested and began to live inside larger cells, benefiting from the protection this gave them. Eventually these bacterial cells became the **mitochondria** that all eukaryote cells now contain. **Chloroplasts** may have arisen in a similar way.

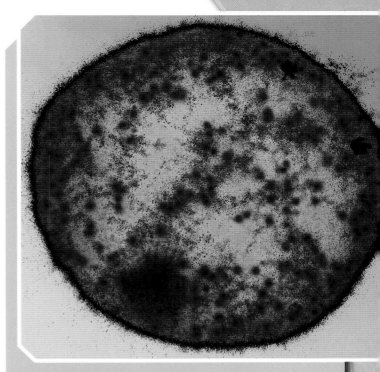

An electron micrograph of the archaea *Methanococcoides burtonii*. Early forms of life may have looked similar to simple bacteria of this sort. Magnification approx. x 120,000.

Once the first eukaryotes appeared, the stage was set for the next great evolutionary step: the emergence of multi-cellular life.

Out of this world cells?

In an experiment that duplicated the harsh conditions of space, including very cold temperatures, no air, and a lot of radiation, scientists managed to get artificial cell membranes to form. The researchers used simple, common compounds, which self-assembled into something that looked very much like a cell membrane. These compounds have been found on dust from meteorites carried to Earth, and years ago they were found to form soapy, water-repelling bubbles. Scientists believe the **molecules** needed to make a cell membrane can be found all over space.

The researchers suggest that organic compounds from interstellar space might have kick-started life on Earth. The scientists are trying to make a model of what might have led to early life by placing **nucleic acids** inside their artificial membranes and feeding them with chemicals known to support cell activity.

The chemistry of life – a summary

The keys to life

1. All life consists of one or more cells.

2. All life is made from the same materials.

3. All life must acquire energy and raw materials to use for growth, to maintain itself, and to reproduce. This process is called **metabolism**.

4. All life can react to changes in its external and internal environments.

5. Instructions for **protein** production coded in **DNA** control the development of multi-cellular organisms and give all life the ability to grow and reproduce.

Carbohydrates, **lipids**, proteins, and **nucleic acids** are the basic ingredients of all cells, the materials that life is built on. All are complex organic compounds called macromolecules – large molecules made up of many smaller repeating units.

Carbohydrates

Carbohydrates contain only the elements carbon, hydrogen, and oxygen.

Simple sugars
These usually have four to six carbons and are used by the cell as an energy source. Glucose is the most common sugar in all cells. Fructose is an important sugar in plant cells. Sucrose, or table sugar, is glucose and fructose joined together.

Polysaccharides
Macromolecules made up of many simple sugar units. For example **starch** is used as an energy store in plants, while plant cell walls are made of **cellulose**. Glycogen is an energy-storing molecule found in animals.

Proteins

Proteins are used as structural materials, for cell movement, for defence against disease, and most importantly for controlling the rates of chemical reactions in cells.

Proteins are made up of long chains of smaller molecules called **amino acids**. Amino acids contain carbon, hydrogen, oxygen, and an extra element, nitrogen. Some amino acids also contain sulphur.

Fibrous proteins
Proteins that form long strands or sheets. Examples are keratin, found in hair and nails, and collagen, found in bone.

Globular proteins
In these proteins the long molecules fold up to make complex three-dimensional shapes. **Enzymes** are globular proteins. Another example is haemoglobin, the protein that carries oxygen in red blood cells.

Lipids

Lipids are molecules containing few oxygen **atoms** and many hydrogen and carbon atoms. They do not dissolve readily in water.

Fats and oils
These compounds are used for energy storage. The fats found in butter and olive oil are examples of this type of lipid.

Phospholipids
These lipids contain the element phosphorus. They are the main structural material of **cell membranes**.

Waxes
Waterproofing materials used to cover leaves and other plant parts above ground.

Cholesterol
One of a group of lipids that are a major part of animal cell membranes.

Nucleic acids

Nucleic acids are formed from chains of smaller molecules called nucleotides. Nucleotides, like amino acids, contain nitrogen. **ATP** is a nucleotide.

DNA
Two linked chains of nucleotides twisted in a double spiral. The instructions for making proteins are encoded in the structure of the DNA molecule.

RNA
Single-chain molecules similar to DNA, but with slightly different nucleotides. One type, **messenger RNA (mRNA)** is formed by transcription of DNA. This mRNA is then translated by RNA and **ribosomes** into amino acid chains, which then become proteins.

Glossary

adenosine triphosphate (ATP) energy-carrying molecule that powers most of the activity in both plant and animal cells

aerobic respiration *see* respiration

algae large group of plant-like protistans, mostly living in water. They range from microscopic single-celled organisms to giant kelp seaweeds.

amino acid naturally occurring chemical used by cells to make proteins

anaerobic respiration *see* respiration

antibiotic chemicals that can destroy or stop the growth of disease-causing bacteria and other micro-organisms

archaea (singular **archaean**) one of two types of prokaryote organism, the other being the bacteria. Once included as part of the bacteria kingdom, the archaea are now considered by many scientists to form a kingdom in their own right. Many of the archaea are found in extreme environments, for example near volcanic vents and in salt lakes. It is for this reason they are often referred to as extremophiles.

atom tiny particle, one of the fundamental particles of matter

bacteria diverse group of prokaryote organisms that are found in almost every part of the Earth. Some can make their own food using light energy, others use chemical energy.

carbohydrate chemical compound composed of carbon, hydrogen, and oxygen. Glucose is a simple carbohydrate.

carotenoids group of pigments found in plants. They give the red colour to autumn leaves.

cell membrane outer boundary of a cell, made of a double layer of lipid and protein molecules

cellulose type of complex carbohydrate forming the cell wall of plant cells

chemosynthesis process in which living things make their own food using chemicals to provide the energy needed. Some bacteria are chemosynthetic.

chlorophyll a light-capturing pigment found in plant cells that is involved in photosynthesis. Chlorophyll gives plants their green colour.

chloroplasts structures found inside plant cells where photosynthesis takes place

chromosome thread-like structure that becomes visible in a cell's nucleus just before it divides. Chromosomes contain a cell's genetic material (DNA).

cilia (singular **cilium**) thin, hair-like structures that project in large numbers from some cells. They are used for movement.

cristae (singular **crista**) folds inside a mitochondrion where some of the enzymes involved in respiration are found

cytomembrane system system of membranes and structures inside a cell that package and distribute newly formed proteins

cytoplasm all of the parts of a cell between the nucleus and the cell membrane

cytoskeleton internal framework of microtubules and other components that supports the cell and moves its organelles around

cytosol fluid or jelly-like part of the cytoplasm that surrounds all the organelles in eukaryote cells

deoxyribonucleic acid (DNA) genetic material found in all cells, by which a living thing passes on its characteristics to the next generation. DNA carries coded instructions for building the cell's many proteins.

diffusion process by which molecules move from one place to another

electron tiny particle within an atom. Electrons form the outside of an atom, orbiting around a central nucleus.

electron microscope *see* microscope

endocytosis process by which a cell takes in a substance by folding the cell membrane around it

endoplasmic reticulum (ER) a network of membranes that run through the cytoplasm of eukaryote cells. Parts of the rough endoplasmic reticulum are covered with ribosomes, which are the site of protein manufacture.

enzyme protein molecule that greatly speeds up a reaction in a cell, or enables the reaction to happen

eukaryote cell that contains a nucleus and other organelles; all cells with the exception of the archaea and bacteria are eukaryote cells

extremophiles another name for the archaea

fermentation type of anaerobic respiration, a means of generating energy from glucose without the use of oxygen

flagella (singular **flagellum**) long, whip-like structure found projecting from the surface of some cells. Flagella are used for movement.

glucose simple carbohydrate, made by plants during photosynthesis and used by all living things as a source of energy in respiration

glycolysis first part of the energy-releasing process in a cell (respiration). It is a series of reactions in which glucose is broken down to two simpler compounds, with a release of energy.

Golgi body structure inside a cell responsible for packaging proteins and other substances manufactured inside the cell ready for export

Krebs cycle part of the chemical process in cells for releasing energy from glucose, fats, and proteins

lactic acid waste product of one form of anaerobic respiration

lipids greasy or oily substances made by cells for creating cell membranes amongst other things. Fats are lipids.

lysosome small membrane-bound structures within cells that contain powerful digestive enzymes. They are used to destroy worn-out organelles or to digest food particles.

Glossary

membrane *see* cell membrane

messenger RNA (mRNA) *see* RNA

metabolism sum total of all the chemical reactions in a cell

microfilaments criss-crossing network of thin fibres attached to the cell membrane, which help give the cell shape

microscope instrument used to make magnified images of small objects. An electron microscope is much more powerful than an optical (light) microscope. It "sees" objects using beams of electrons instead of light rays.

microtubules protein tubes that are used by the cell to move things about. They are part of the cytoskeleton.

mitochondria (singular **mitochondrion**) structure within the cell where aerobic respiration takes place. Mitochondria produce most of a cell's energy.

molecules particles made up of two or more atoms joined together

nucleic acid class of very large molecules found in living cells that includes DNA and RNA

nucleolus part of the nucleus where segments of chromosomes are unwound so their DNA can be "read" in order to make messenger RNA. This RNA is used to make ribosomes, where proteins are put together.

nucleus large, membrane-bound structure in the centre of a eukaryote cell where its genetic material is held

organelle structure within cells, often bound by a membrane, that carries out a specific task or tasks

organism any kind of living thing

osmosis movement of water across a partially permeable membrane (such as a cell membrane) from a less concentrated solution to a more concentrated one

parasite organism that lives on or in another organism and gets food from it without giving anything in return

photosynthesis process by which green plants and some other organisms use the energy of sunlight to make sugars (food) from carbon dioxide and water

phytoplankton single-celled, water-dwelling organisms that are capable of photosynthesis

plasma membrane another term for cell membrane

plasmid piece of DNA, usually circular, found inside a bacterium

predator organism that catches and eats other organisms for food. The organisms that a predator eats are called its prey.

prokaryote type of cell that does not have its genetic material in a nucleus. The archaea and bacteria are prokaryotes.

proteins complex organic molecules that perform a variety of essential tasks in cells, such as providing structure and acting as catalysts (enzymes) in chemical reactions

protistans diverse grouping of organisms, most of them microscopic and single-celled

protozoan a protistan that is similar to an animal in that it cannot make its own food but has to "eat"

respiration breaking down of complex molecules in living cells to release energy. This is the main way by which cells get their energy. Aerobic respiration requires oxygen, while anaerobic respiration, a less efficient process, does not.

ribosome structure in the cell where proteins are put together from amino acids

RNA (ribonucleic acid) nucleic acid, similar to DNA, which is involved in the process of protein manufacture. Messenger RNA is made from DNA in the nucleus, and acts as a template for making proteins on the ribosomes.

spore extremely small reproductive body produced by fungi and some other living things

starch complex carbohydrate, used as a food store in plants

vacuole fluid-filled cavity inside a cell that is surrounded by a membrane

vesicle tiny membrane sac used, for example, in transporting proteins in a cell

virus non-living agent composed of DNA or RNA with an outer protein layer that is capable of infecting a cell and using its machinery to make copies of itself

Further reading and websites

Books

Cells and Life Processes, Denise Walker (Evans Brothers, 2006)

Life Processes: Cells and Systems, Holly Wallace (Heinemann Library, 2006)

Life Processes: Classification, Holly Wallace (Heinemann Library, 2006)

Microlife series: four books about the world of micro-organisms

        The Benefits of Bacteria, Robert Snedden (Heinemann Library, 2007)

        Fighting Infectious Disease, Robert Snedden (Heinemann Library, 2007)

        Scientists and Discoveries, Robert Snedden (Heinemann Library, 2007)

        A World of Micro-organisms, Robert Snedden (Heinemann Library, 2007)

Websites

Cells Alive (http://www.cellsalive.com/)
        A good introduction to the cell, with homework help.

Micro-organisms (www.biology4kids.com/files/micro_main.html)
        Lots of clearly presented information on the world of micro-organisms.

Meet the Microbes (www.microbeworld.org/microbes)
        An introduction to micro-organisms and the people who study them.

Index